UNDER THE WILD WESTERN SKY

Library of Congress Cataloging-in-Publication Data is available.
ISBN 0-688-17121-4 — ISBN 0-688-17122-2 (lib. bdg.)

Typography by Stephanie Bart-Horvath
1 2 3 4 5 6 7 8 9 10
❖
First Edition

UNDER THE WILD WESTERN SKY

JIM ARNOSKY

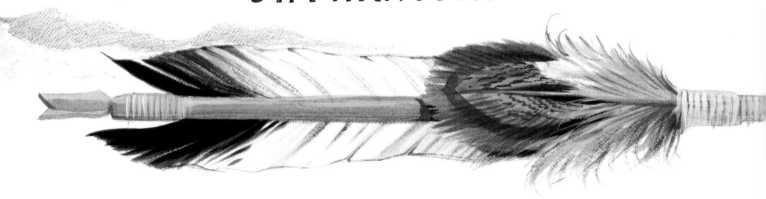

HarperCollins*Publishers*

For Holton and Jane

INTRODUCTION

On four separate journeys to find and study wild animals, my wife, Deanna, and I have traveled west of the Mississippi River, west of the Rocky Mountains, into the canyon lands and deserts. We have spent whole days outdoors, from sunrise to sunset, in the windy freedom of wide-open spaces. Deanna photographed. I videotaped and sketched. Mostly we enjoyed discovering America together and feeling at home wherever we happened to be.

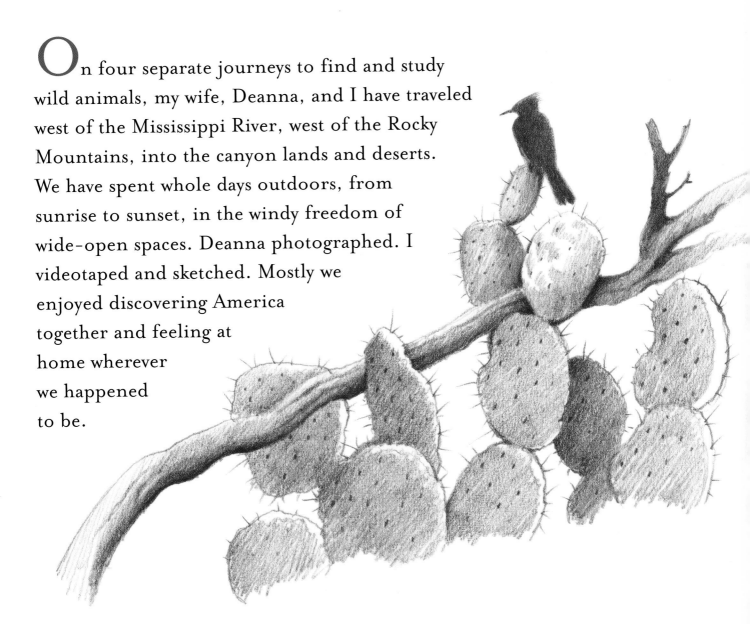

This book is a collection of some of our favorite places. Deanna and I are ready to see them all again and show them to you! So saddle up and ride along as we wander through big country, exploring the life and awesome landscape under the wild western sky.

Phoenix, Arizona, is a city in the heart of the Sonoran Desert. All around Phoenix the hill country is covered with brush, small trees, and gigantic saguaro (pronounced *swarro*) cactuses. The big hot sun was going down as I took a long walk down a well-worn trail that led through wild land.

Peccary

In the dust were many tiny hoofprints of the small wild desert pig known as the peccary. I hoped to spot one, but there was none to be found. The only wildlife I saw were Gambel's quail running in bunches on the darkening ground or flying close together in the twilight.

In daylight the Gambel's quail is a strikingly beautiful bird.

Saguaro cactus

Prickly pear cactus

Cactus wren

Cholla cactus

Beavertail

Organ-pipe cactus

Barrel cactus

Wherever we paused to rest, I sat with
my notepad and sketched the cactus.

On our walks together in the desert, Deanna and I tried to identify all the different cactus plants we saw. The largest was the saguaro cactus. Some grow twenty-five feet tall and weigh a ton or more.

The ground around a giant saguaro is often crowded with many smaller varieties of cactus. My favorite is the prickly pear cactus, which grows in clusters that can spread ten feet high and ten feet wide, creating a whole prickly pear cactus wall.

The cactuses I have painted are the ones most commonly seen. Learn these, and the desert landscape becomes a more familiar and inviting place.

Coachwhip cactus

The more at home we felt in the desert, the more often we had to remind ourselves to be careful. While exploring in a lush green arroyo, we came upon many small crevices where snakes could hide. In one crevice we spotted a large, recently shed snakeskin. The scales were smooth and not ridged like a rattler's. I believe the shed skin was that of a king snake.

King snakes are constrictors that regularly feed on other snakes, including rattlesnakes.

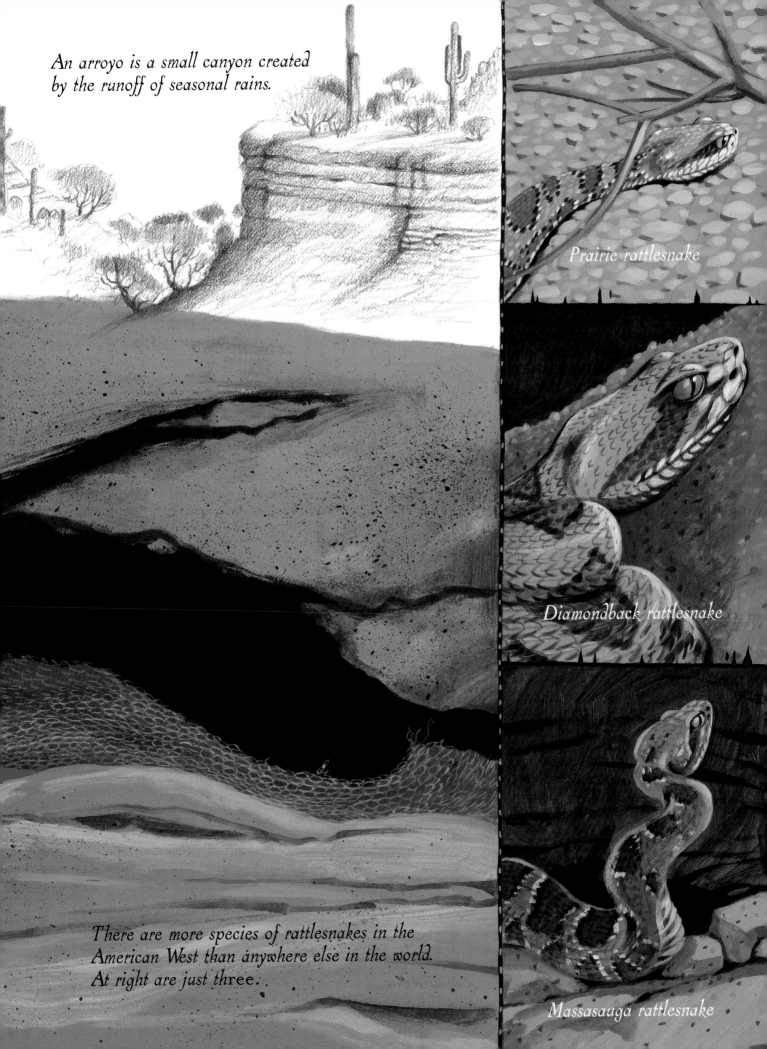

An arroyo is a small canyon created
by the runoff of seasonal rains.

Prairie rattlesnake

Diamondback rattlesnake

There are more species of rattlesnakes in the
American West than anywhere else in the world.
At right are just three.

Massasauga rattlesnake

The western landscape is so spectacular, your eyes can barely take it in. You have to take time and look awhile to really see all that is before you. I had been admiring the distant sunlit cliffs for some minutes before I noticed the bald eagle perched on a shadowed snag just a hundred feet away!

Then and there I was reminded to "cover" every scene with my eyes the same way I'd paint the scene with a brush—beginning with the sky, then taking in the distant landforms, the mid-range areas, and finally the foreground. By looking at scenery this way, I spotted high soaring birds, cattle grazing on distant hills, small animals hiding in nearby brush, and lizards dashing by my feet.

Lesser earless lizard

Desert cottontail

All over the West, Deanna had to pull me away from ranches and cattle and horses and cowboys. She reminded me that we were supposed to be looking for wildlife. On a cold and windy day, we took a long walk around a lake stained pink from Oklahoma's red soil. Deanna wanted to see if any sandhill cranes were resting here on their way south to Texas or Mexico for the winter. These cranes were wading in the shallow water on the far side of the lake. We also saw our very first American wigeons.

American wigeons

In far western Oklahoma we saw this scissor-tailed flycatcher—another new bird for us.

Sandhill cranes

While driving through the Oklahoma prairie, we counted dozens of red-tailed hawks. The nutrient-rich prairie grasses support an abundance of rodents, lizards, and snakes that the hawks prey upon. On one particular morning there were more hawks on the ground covering fresh kills than there were perched on high wires or fence posts. Rain was coming, and the hawks were feeding heavily before the storm.

I thought the prairie red-tailed hawks looked larger than our red-tailed hawks back East. They may be. Or the western hawks may just have been fluffing their feathers against the ever-present prairie winds.

Red-tailed hawk on Oklahoma's
Tall Grass Prairie Preserve

Their scientific name is bison, but to Deanna and me they will always be buffalo. We've seen buffalo in private herds on farms and ranches. We have always wanted to see them on a western preserve where they still can roam. The Wichita Mountains National Wildlife Refuge is just such a place. There you can see buffalo as wild as they can be.

Deanna photographed this big bull resting on a rocky slope. An adult buffalo stands six and a half feet tall at the shoulders. Even though this one was lying down, it was the most impressive creature we have ever seen.

To get her prairie dog portraits, Deanna knelt outside a burrow and waited for the occupants to pop up.

The herds of buffalo that we saw did not stay where we found them for very long. They moved from place to place across the refuge. We drove the winding refuge road searching for their tracks, hoping to see and photograph more. At one place buffalo tracks led through a large prairie dog community. When we walked through, the vibrations of our footsteps brought many of the "townspeople" out to have a look at us. As the curious little animals popped up out of hole after hole, I wondered how the burrow-riddled ground must have trembled when the buffalo walked over it!

Everywhere in our travels we saw reminders of the West of long ago. A hand-painted buffalo skull depicting an old hunt. An arrow quiver hanging on a museum wall. Flint arrowheads found embedded in a stream bank.

Arrows and quiver made by a Navajo artisan

We even saw a smoothed-out spot in the prairie where buffalo once rolled and wallowed in the mud. Besides seeing all these things, Deanna and I met people from the Navajo, Cheyenne, Kiowa, Choctaw, Chickasaw, Comanche, Pawnee, Cherokee, and Arapaho tribes—descendants of the original westerners.

Flint arrowheads

An ancient buffalo wallow

Today's West is rich in history and tradition. History needs to be shared, and tradition passed down. In homes, schools, and museums, at Native American powwows and ceremonial tribal dances, on ranches and rodeo grounds, we found the fires of history and tradition burning brightly. And in the great refuges and vast preserves, we saw wildlife and wild lands we both had dreamed of seeing since childhood. Our dreams became reality under the wild western sky.

The drawings in this book were done in soft pencil.
The paintings were painted with acrylics. I kept the
brush loaded with more paint than water to create the
look of oils. Feel free to copy all the illustrations,
using your own favorite medium.

Jim Arnosky